VINTAGE BUSES IN GLORIOUS DEVON

A JOURNEY IN COLOUR

ROGER MALONE

Pen & Sword
TRANSPORT

AN IMPRINT OF PEN & SWORD BOOKS LTD
YORKSHIRE - PHILADELPHIA

First published in Great Britain in 2019 by
Pen and Sword Transport
An imprint of
Pen & Sword Books Ltd
Yorkshire - Philadelphia

ISBN 978 1 52674 831 7

Typeset by Aura Technology and Software Services, India

Printed and bound in China through Printworks Global Ltd.

Pen & Sword Books Ltd incorporates the Imprints of Pen & Sword Books Archaeology, Atlas, Aviation, Battleground, Discovery, Family History, History, Maritime, Military, Naval, Politics, Railways, Select, Transport, True Crime, Fiction, Frontline Books, Leo Cooper, Praetorian Press, Seaforth Publishing, Wharncliffe and White Owl.

For a complete list of Pen & Sword titles please contact

PEN & SWORD BOOKS LIMITED
47 Church Street, Barnsley, South Yorkshire, S70 2AS, England
E-mail: enquiries@pen-and-sword.co.uk
Website: www.pen-and-sword.co.uk

or

PEN AND SWORD BOOKS
1950 Lawrence Rd, Havertown, PA 19083, USA
E-mail: Uspen-and-sword@casematepublishers.com
Website: www.penandswordbooks.com

CONTENTS

INTRODUCTION

It is said you can wait ages for a bus – and then three come along at once. Well, in Glorious Devon, if you're lucky, a lot more than that could come along. The county is fortunate in not only being blessed with some spectacular scenery, but also with an array of events featuring vintage transport.

This book is a pictorial endeavour to celebrate both. Climb aboard as we take an armchair journey, travelling from coast to coast, with a nostalgic array of preserved buses and coaches. So, tickets please, and off we go.

Each year in South Devon, for one day only, there is an almost surreal abundance of vintage buses. The Kingsbridge Vintage Bus Running Day sends the clock spinning back to the glory days of public transport. Centred on the town's bus station, a virtual merry-go-round of more than 40 preserved buses and coaches delight the public with a nostalgic reincarnation of the past.

Created in 2007 by Colin Billington, chairman of the Thames Valley and Great Western Omnibus Trust, the event has grown in success year by year. It attracts hundreds of bus enthusiasts and members of the public who come to enjoy travelling on preserved vehicles from a bygone age.

Destinations range out from Kingsbridge, across the South Hams' fibrous network of roads, north to Totnes, east towards Dartmouth and west to Bigbury-on-Sea. One of the most popular runs with passengers has been out along the coastal strip of Slapton Sands and on to the sheltered bay at Blackpool Sands. However, in the 2018 event, the route had to be abandoned beyond Slapton village because coastal erosion temporarily caused this vulnerable part of the A379 to close.

Kingsbridge Vintage Bus Running Day has much to attract the visitor – whether wishing to remain in the town's hub of transport activity or choosing to head off to some of the attractive destinations. There is certainly no finer sight than an example of heritage transport arriving at an Agatha Christie-esque coastal setting, with all the atmosphere which that evokes.

On such occasions, one has to admire the skill and iron nerve of the drivers who take the serpentine Devon lanes in their stride. Being in charge of crash-gear buses, burrowing their way through deep, hedge-lined narrows to finally emerge at the seaside, is not a driving experience for the faint-hearted.

In the days when such buses ran normal services to South Hams coastal honey pots like Hope Cove, Thurlestone, Bantham and Bigbury-on-Sea, seasonal traffic was nothing like the level it has become. Holiday makers completing the last leg of their journey invariably arrived by bus or taxi from the nearest railway station! A minority might have journeyed by car – while the even more privileged could have been conveyed in the luxury of a chauffeur-driven limousine. Certainly, the risk of a log-jam of weekender 4x4 drivers, ill-versed in the dark art of reverse, would have been unheard of. Today, unfortunately, carefree empty summer lanes are but a sepia memory.

'You must take command of the road,' Colin Billington advises any busmen new to steering their noble steeds out into a slice of rural Devon.

And they do. Drivers can occasionally be seen sitting in their cab with an inscrutable expression, hands resting patiently on the wheel. The vehicle that has had the misfortune to meet the bus, radiator to radiator, at the wrong moment is obliged to reverse back until it can squeeze into a convenient passing spot. Such impasses can elicit wry amusement from the coach passengers, and chagrin from the unfortunate motorist wrestling with reverse. However, most, surprised to suddenly confront a half-cab apparition from the 1940s, hopefully see it as a small price to pay for getting up close and personal with a unique piece of transport history.

While Kingsbridge offers an annual autumnal delight in the daylight, for five years a more nocturnal event operated out of Exeter's Paris Street Bus and Coach Station. The Twilight Running was created by Dan Shears in 2010 to mark 40 years since the demise of Exeter Corporation Transport when the council sold it to the state-owned National Bus Company in 1970. The last bus ran into the depot around 23.30 on 31 March and on the next day, 1 April, it was absorbed by local NBC subsidiary Devon General. This was an irony not wasted on Dan, as Stagecoach, which sponsored his event, had bought out Devon General years later in 1996.

Dan is an engineer and bus enthusiast, whose late father Colin Shears created what is now known as the West of England Transport Collection, at Winkleigh in Mid-Devon. The first Exeter event was dogged by a predicted, and accurate, weather forecast of rain. Ironically, far from putting a damper on proceedings, the inclement conditions enhanced the atmosphere for both passengers and photographers.

Like phantoms from the past, vehicles exuded a charming, mellow inner glow as condensation and old-style light bulbs worked their magic. Out of the ten buses taking part, all but one were former Exeter City Transport vehicles, and four of those were owned by Dan.

The oldest bus running was a 1938 Leyland 'Tiger' half-cab single decker – purchased for preservation by Colin Shears in 1956. One of a small batch, with special open-platform and extra luggage capacity for use at Exeter St David's railway station, it was then used on Exeter City Transport route K, and country destinations. Letters, instead of numbers, were used to differentiate between Exeter City Transport routes and those operated by Devon General.

This, and other lovingly restored vehicles, turned the heads of admiring pre-Christmas shoppers as they radiated out from the city centre's bus station in Paris Street along Sidwell Street and High Street. Services also operated out to the suburbs of Hill Barton, Crossmead, Pennsylvania, Redhills and the village of Broadclyst.

In 2016 both Exeter and Plymouth's Bretonside bus and coach stations were due for closure. To lament their demise, and provide one last hurrah, a convoy of coaches ran from Exeter to Plymouth on Saturday, 16 July. Following much of the old A38, the cavalcade travelled through Chudleigh, Ashburton and Buckfastleigh en route to Plymouth. Here, such one-time familiar Bretonside visitors as Royal Blue, Grey Cars and Devon General swelled the parked ranks of preserved former Plymouth City Transport vehicles.

Beneath a cloudless summer sky, a piece of heritage history unfurled as, for one last time, Bretonside relived the sort of bustle it had enjoyed in its heyday. Ironically, while this marked the closure of Bretonside, Exeter was to enjoy a brief reprieve.

Sadly, however, the inevitable finally happened. On Saturday, 16 June 2018, after several false final curtain calls, the coach part of Exeter Bus and Coach Station closed for redevelopment.

As it happened, the date coincided with the year's annual outing of Royal Blues. Once the leading long-distance express coach operator in the South and West of England, these distinctive vehicles represented the acme of opulent coach travel. As part of the 2018 run, on this occasion heading along former routes towards Ilfracombe and on to Minehead, the ten-strong Royal Blues made a special detour to salute the coach station's passing into the history books.

The tour was organised by Colin Billington and, one by one, the coaches rolled into the now empty coach park. It was fitting that Colin's 1951 Royal Blue Bristol LL6B half-cab, the oldest vehicle in the convoy, had the poignant distinction of being the very last coach to drive away from the now deserted area.

While this was by way of a transport wake, making a date for happier reasons later in 2018 was a celebration of the type of public transport Tavistock bus station would have experienced half a century previously. Organised by the Thames Valley and Great Western Omnibus Trust, it recreated the local bus scene of 1968 with services to Lydford, across the Tamar to Calstock on the Cornish side of the river, and up across Dartmoor to Princetown – 1,430 feet above sea level.

While passengers rode the buses back in 1968, hit-makers riding the pop charts that year included The Beatles, Beach Boys, Bee Gees – and Mary Hopkin singing 'Those Were The Days' which, in retrospect, could be the ironic bus nostalgists' lament.

Along with once ubiquitous Western National and Southern National buses in their familiar Tilling green livery, the county also sported another colour – that of the distinctive maroon and cream of Devon General which from 1919 was the principal operator in South Devon, reaching down as far as Totnes and the Dart. Although the main depots were in Exeter and Torquay, the company's routes covered most of both east and mid-Devon, with vehicles ranging as far afield as Plymouth, Minehead and Weymouth. Fortunately, representatives of these companies are happily preserved and can be enjoyed taking part in the various heritage events.

Another familiar sight on Devon roads was local independent coach operator Grey Cars. The business was purchased by A. Timpson & Sons of Catford in 1931 and passed to Devon General the following year. Most Devon General coaches continued to operate under Grey Cars' name. Representatives of this one-time Torquay-based fleet put in regular appearances at the county' s popular beauty spots. Their grey, maroon and cream livery was always a smart visual signature of this highly-popular coach operator. In that halcyon era of day trips, Grey Cars would take holidaymakers off for cream teas to Widecombe-in-the-Moor, mystery tours, and evening trips to country pubs.

In 2013, a centenary of service was celebrated by Grey Cars with an outing of preserved coaches setting out for Dartmouth from the modern-day company's headquarters at Heathfield, Bovey Tracey. The splendid line-up of Grey Cars along the harbour side at Dartmouth was a pleasant reminder of times when these coaches were regular bringers of tourists and additional business to such popular Devon towns.

Moving inland to Winkleigh, in the heart of Devon, there is the West of England Transport Collection. This is not open to the public, except on specific operating days. It was here, in 1963, that Colin Shears (1935-2016) acquired grounds on an old Second World War airfield, once the home of RAF Winkleigh, which used to host Beaufighter and Mosquito night fighters. With spacious off-road running, and a sizeable ex-Second

World War aircraft hangar, Colin was able to house his own vehicles and rent out space to other owners.

Colin kindly showed me around on my first visit. It was like a Bermuda Triangle of buses lost to the outside world. Some, stored outdoors, had succumbed to the vagaries of the elements and the clawing stranglehold of brambles. Some were preserved but far from pristine. Frozen in time, with faded liveries and frayed interiors, they were waiting their turn – moth-balled in limbo for the immediate future. Others, at the end of the preservation process, glinted under lovingly applied final coats of gloss.

The commitment involved to restore a wreck of an old bus was starkly evident. Reversing the fortunes of some rescued vehicles clearly requires a major investment of both commitment and cash. Colin, who felt the best way to describe himself was a 'passenger transport collection custodian', originally dreamed of creating a museum but found there was no help and little interest. However, he contented himself with the fact he was instrumental in saving a veritable fleet of buses.

'The enthusiast has a feeling for these vehicles but the general public don't seem to,' he told me at the time. 'If there were more bus enthusiasts, more buses would have been saved.'

With railway preservation capturing people's imagination, Colin said 30 years ago a bus enthusiast wasn't thought to be much by the general public. As a result, much that could have been saved was scrapped. 'Now it is different, because historical things have gained more interest from the general public. But without the work carried out by the West of England Transport Collection, 80 per cent of the older vehicles here would not have been saved.'

Colin's journey from boy enthusiast to bus benefactor was a lengthy labour of love throughout most of his 81 years. Born and raised in Exeter, he was first captivated by the way the old Exeter City Transport double deckers seemed to tower above him.

'In school, when I should have been listening to lessons, I was more interested in listening out for the engines of the buses passing outside,' he said. With the honed ears of a musician who is pitch perfect, Colin could identify many of the buses' mechanical signature tune merely by their engine tone. 'They all had character and made a lot of noise which I liked. The Leyland had a distinctive whine that was like a siren!'

The running of the collection is now in the safe hands of Colin's son Dan who, at the last count, has some 40 vintage vehicles in his care. On open days, courtesy of Dan and his team of fellow enthusiasts, the village of Winkleigh has enjoyed the best public transport service in Britain – with buses passing through the square every five minutes.

Other Winkleigh outings have taken passengers on free rides to the Winkleigh Cider factory, and along the lanes to Eggesford Station – the nearest rail connection. Timings were arranged so the services made connections with the Exeter-Barnstaple trains on the Tarka Line.

As well as the West of England Transport Collection housing buses with regional links to the area, Dan has acquired a collection of former Bournemouth vehicles. His yellow-liveried Bournemouth Transport 1950 Leyland PD2 double decker has not only been a colourful sight around Winkleigh village, but occasionally takes part in bus rallies further afield.

'I think people like the old buses because they have such a distinct character. There is something about driving one – everybody looks,' says Dan.

My own interest in buses began as a schoolboy because it was my daily transport. The homeward run on a rainy winter's day, seated in the top deck, held a particular charm. The interior was bathed in its own mellow glow. Through the window, street lamps and shop fronts reflected in the wet sheen of the streets. Condensation inside, and rivulets of rain outside, turned everything beyond the bus into ripples of watery wonder.

Sown here, unwittingly, were the first seeds of nostalgia. For all of us, the seductive power of warmly recalled images are hard to resist. Fortunately, pro-active enthusiasts put such pangs to practical use, helping to save and secure vehicles from the golden age of public transport. That today we can see so many preserved buses is in itself a minor miracle. Railways always stole the limelight with the romance of steam-hauled expresses. An irony when you consider that, for most people, buses had a more visual presence.

Maybe, that was it. Used for getting to and from the daily grind, the humble bus was unlikely to be elevated beyond being just a means to an end. Uncelebrated due to its utilitarian ubiquity, it was taken for granted when it arrived on time, and cursed when it didn't. Only with hindsight have we come to fully appreciate and admire these workhorses of the road, along with their more leisure-orientated stablemates, the touring coach. Without the foresight and dedication of those who saved them there would be so much less left to look at – and to photograph.

All the images of heritage transport on Devon roads were taken over the past ten years. I have not dated pictures except in specific circumstances. There are other vintage books that excellently date and detail such vehicles – having recorded them operating in their revenue-earning, often rarely photographed, heyday.

I can make no such claim when photographing the lovingly preserved survivors from the past now enjoying celebrity status in the present. My aim has simply been to picture them in locations that conjure as timeless a quality as possible. It is good fortune that there are still so many delightful locations in Devon, such as Hope Cove, or the stretch along Slapton Sands, that have altered comparatively little down the decades.

I sincerely hope you enjoy travelling through these pages as much as I have enjoyed the journey of putting them together.

TORBAY

In what was once an everyday sight along Torquay's seafront, AEC Regent V, CTT 513C, resplendent in Devon General livery, heads towards Paignton with a glimpse of Torre Abbey Sands to the right.

Plenty of sea air for passengers on the top deck, as 1934 AEC Regent, OD 7497, heads for Paignton. This vehicle is the only survivor of the group of six Regents that were converted to form the first fleet of open toppers for Devon General Sea Front Service. Torquay is in the background and the Princess Theatre can be seen on the shoreline near the zig-zag footpath to the left.

With sea, sand and beach huts in the background, Bournemouth Corporation 1960 Leyland Titan PD3, 8159 EL, looks as at home in Torbay as it would in its old Hampshire, now Dorset, coastal stomping ground.

Straying from Putney Heath is London Transport 1951 Leyland Titan 7RT, LYF 104, as it drives along the Torquay seafront.

The English Riviera would be nothing without its palm trees and here, framed by one in Torquay, 1946 Devon General AEC Regal, HTT 487, heads away from The Strand towards Princess Gardens.

Straying from its City of Plymouth routes, Leyland Titan PD2 *Sir Francis Drake*, MCO 658, takes a turn past the clifftop gardens of The Downs at Babbacombe. The popular Babbacombe Theatre is just visible between the trees.

Adjacent to the bustling resort of Torquay, St Marychurch still manages to retain a particular timelessness. Here, open top 1965 Leyland PD3, BUF 425C, owned by Andrew James Quality Travel, waits for passengers in Babbacombe Road, St Marychurch. Bygones museum can be seen behind with St Mary's Church in the background.

Passing The Downs at Babbacombe, and overlooking the bay beyond, is Devon General AEC Regent, OD 7497, in open-top colours – a reversal of the company's normal maroon and cream livery.

The Agatha Christie bus, AC1, 1947 Leyland Tiger half-cab, AHL 694, passes the ornate Lodge and enters the drive leading to Greenway, the famous Devon authors' summer home, on the banks of the River Dart. It has been a National Trust property since 2000.

BUCKFASTLEIGH

Side by side, Southern National and Western National are sharing duties at Buckfastleigh Station on the South Devon Railway. Built in 1951, Bristol LWL5G, LTA 772, was originally a Western National vehicle. It was transferred to Southern National in 1960 and was based at Weymouth depot. Built in 1933, Bristol H, FJ 8967, was rebodied in 1942, and was a South Devon vehicle until withdrawn in 1957.

It's a particularly peaceful Sunday in 'down town' Ashburton. Bristol LWL5G waits, just past the Bull Ring, in West Street before heading back to Buckfastleigh.

The Church House Inn, Holne, is the turning point for Bristol H, FJ 8967, with Colin Billington behind the wheel, as it prepares to return to Buckfastleigh.

A regular source of vintage transport from Buckfastleigh Station to Buckfast Abbey is this splendid example of a London Transport 1964 AEC RM, ALD 872B. Incongruous in Devon perhaps but, nevertheless, a delightful slice of nostalgia.

Waiting to pick up passengers who have visited Buckfast Abbey, a popular tourist attraction that forms part of an active Benedictine monastery.

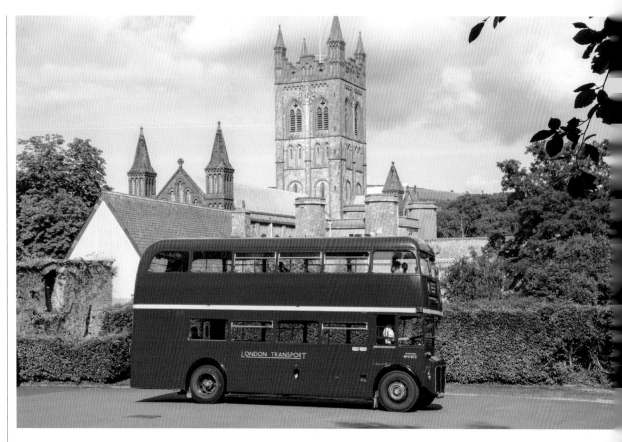

The bus negotiates the narrow confines of Buckfastleigh's Fore Street. Owned by the South Devon Railway, it has been restored to 1960s LT style.

EAST DEVON

1953 Leyland Titan PD2/12, RTC 822, originally owned by Rawtenstall Corporation, now by Quantock Heritage, parks up on Sidmouth esplanade with the red sandstone cliffs of Peak Hill in the background.

Heading into the Regency town between the thatched properties of Station Road is Bristol RELHG6, OTA 632G, on a Royal Blue run to Devon. Delivered new in 1968 to Southern National as a Royal Blue coach, it was based mainly in the North Devon area.

This is as close to the Sidmouth seafront as this Royal Blue cavalcade gets. 1953 Bristol LS6G, OTT 98, has just come around the triangle where regular bus services arrive and turn, and passes Crossville CRG106, AFM 106G.

East Kent TD5, GFN 273, departs from Sidmouth for Exeter along Station Road – a legacy from the days when the town had a station. The coach was built as a double deck TD5 in 1938 and was rebodied by Beadle in 1952. Withdrawn in 1967, it passed into preservation in 1972.

Under a cloudless summer sky, Crossville CRG106 descends Coastguard Hill into the genteel East Devon resort of Budleigh Salterton.

A perfect pair – 1951 Bristol LL6B, LTA 729, passes 1961 Bristol MW6G, 56 GUO, as it takes a break by the beach at Budleigh Salterton. Both carry the destination 'Exmouth' – the next leg of their journey.

An early Sunday morning and the streets of Honiton are deserted except for a convoy of Royal Blues led by Bristol L6B, EMW 284. Delivered to Wilts and Dorset in 1947 it was initially allocated to their Salisbury depot. The coach was sold in 1962 and entered preservation in 1986.

Heading past the War Memorial in Honiton's High Street is 1953 Bristol LS6G, OTT 98. Entering service new in 1953 with Southern National Omnibus Company in Royal Blue livery for express services, it was transferred to Western National in 1969. It entered preservation in 1972.

The tide is out on the vast expanse of the Exe Estuary as 1980 Bristol VR, LFJ 862W, travels along the Royal Avenue at Exmouth.

Open top 1961 Leyland Atlantean, 931 GTA, former Devon General Sea Dog *Sir Thomas Howard*, sports an unmissable advert while providing passengers with a bracing view of the Exe Estuary. This is an overall advertising livery based on the National Bus Company red livery of the 1970s.

1946 AEC Regal, HTT 487, heads through Woodbury on a round trip from Exmouth in the rain. A representative of Devon General's post-war single deck fleet, it was found derelict in a field in East Devon before being saved and restored by Ron Greet.

Bournemouth Corporation 1956 Leyland Tiger Cub, RRU 903, pulls past The Church on the Green at Budleigh Salterton. It has had a brief stop in Station Road. But alas, just like Sidmouth, the town no longer has a station.

There is a lovely sense of summer with tourists and bunting in Budleigh Salterton High Street as Bournemouth Corporation's buttercup yellow livery brings its own added dash of sunshine.

GREY CARS

Leading the centenary party for Grey Cars is London Transport 1964 AEC RM, ALD 872B, heading towards Newton Abbot station.

Making the connection to pick up passengers from Newton Abbot station is Grey Cars 1964 AEC Reliance, 1 RDV, and 1950 AEC Regal III, LTA 629. At the rear is a 1964 AEC Reliance Harrington coach, 100 VRL.

Revisiting old haunts on the company's centenary birthday outing, 1963 AEC Reliance and 1950 AEC Regal III pass The Downs, Babbacombe, with the arc of Babbacombe Bay in the distance.

Heading down Torwood Street towards the centre of Torquay, Grey Cars 1962 AEC Reliance passes AEC Reliance Harrington Cavalier, which has parked near the site of the former Grey Cars garage, now a bowling alley. This coach entered service with Hawkey's Tours of Newquay in 1964.

A splendid trio of Grey Cars line up along the Embankment at Dartmouth.

Grey Cars 1950 AEC Regal III passes the historic Dartmouth station, located on the town's river front, and opened in 1864. Passengers arriving here had to cross by ferry to Kingswear in order to catch a train. It was closed by British Railways in 1972 and the attractive building, with its canopy and decorative iron work, is now a restaurant.

Under the watchful eye of the houses across the River Dart at Kingswear, a Grey Cars coach skirts the inner harbour.

London Transport 1964 AEC RM heads towards local landmark York House, an imposing Grade II listed mock Tudor Victorian building at the corner of Spithead and South Embankment.

Having dropped its passengers, Grey Cars AEC Reliance, 1 RDV, is parked beneath the impressive architecture of Abbey Church in the grounds of Buckfast Abbey, an active Benedictine monastery near Buckfastleigh. It has been taking part in a Devon Coastal Run.

DAWLISH AND TEIGNMOUTH

Eastbourne Corporation AEC Regent III, AHC 442, new to the town's transport fleet in 1950, passes through the centre of Dawlish showing off its splendid livery. Nice that the man walking his dog had a colour coordinated tee shirt!

Devon General 1980 Bristol VRT in National Bus Company livery, LFJ 862W, crosses the Brook in the centre of town. In the forefront is one of the famous black swans which have been residents here since the early 1900s.

Devon General AEC Regent V, CTT 518C, new in 1965, heads through the centre of Dawlish with The Lawn behind, en route to Teignmouth.

The Regent V descends West Cliff to enter Dawlish. It spent most of its working life based at Exmouth depot and was withdrawn from service in 1978.

1956 AEC Regent V, ROD 765, waits at the bus stop at Dawlish with the famous and precarious West of England main line and Dawlish station immediately behind.

Devon General
KOD 585, an AEC Regent III with Weymann body, pulls away from a stop at Dawlish. It was delivered late in 1949 but entered service in 1950 on Exeter city services. It was withdrawn in 1961.

A drive along the seafront at Teignmouth is in store for the passengers aboard Devon General AEC Regent V, CTT 513C.

1952 AEC Regent III, NTT 661, squeezes through Hollands Road into Regent Street as it heads towards the seafront.

Withdrawn from service in 1965, 1952 AEC Regent III is a splendid sight as it curves into Den Crescent, advertising the delights of Grey Cars as it goes.

Taking part in the Devon Coastal Run, organised by the Historic Transport Club, is 1950 Bedford OB Duple Vista coach, BJV 590, parked at Teignmouth Promenade with the inviting blue waters of Torbay beyond.

This intriguing 1940 Leyland Titan TD7, HF 9126, arriving at Teignmouth Promenade was originally a Wallasey Corporation double decker. In the early 1950s, it was converted to a mobile control unit. Here it is taking part in the annual Devon Coastal Run which begins at Exeter Racecourse and ends in Bovey Tracey.

Sunshine and sunshades on the seafront as Bristol LL6B, LTA 958, enjoys the holiday atmosphere at Teignmouth. The coach was operated by Southern National from 1951 to 1964.

1952 Bedford MLC, FFX 458, was built to the special order of Dorset County Council education committee by Lee Motors of Bournemouth. A regular visitor to the Devon Coastal Run, it is parked in the company of a 1959 Ford Thames Trader.

A long way from its original stomping ground is Eastbourne Corporation 1936 Leyland Titan TD4, JK 5605, which was converted to an open top bus the early 1950s and named *White Ensign*. Appropriately enough it is by the seaside – with Teignmouth Pier in the background.

Originally used by Grimsby Town Football Club to tour around the country, the 1950 Bedford OB Duple Vista coach now in Taw & Torridge 'colours' crosses the River Teign and heads towards Shaldon.

PLYMOUTH HOE

Plymouth Hoe has proved a spectacular location for this annual event hosted by the Plymouth City Transport Preservation Group. The tall stand-alone Mayflower Post Hotel at the end of The Hoe has since been demolished.

Bournemouth Corporation 1960 Leyland Titan PD3, 8159 EL, faces the Plymouth Naval Memorial, which bears the names of approximately 23,000 British and Commonwealth sailors who were lost in both world wars.

Leyland Atlantean
Henry Winstanley, STK 131T, named after the builder of the first lighthouse on the Eddystone Rocks in 1698, 13 miles south-west of Plymouth, stands in the shadow of the famous city landmark of Smeaton's Tower. This was the third lighthouse to be built, remaining until erosion of rocks caused it to be replaced by a fourth lighthouse in 1882 which still stands today. Smeaton's Tower was dismantled and re-erected on The Hoe as a memorial and is now a tourist attraction.

The rain has passed and the sun is out as 'Sea Dog' Atlantean *Sir Martin Frobisher*, 724 XUW, waits for custom.

One of the Plymouth Citybus company's heritage vehicles, this Leyland Titan PD2, *Sir Francis Drake,* entered service with Plymouth City Transport in 1956. It was converted to open top after being damaged in the bus wash and has had many different liveries.

With the blue water of Plymouth Sound and Drake's Island in the background, 1980-built Bristol VRT, LFJ 844W, looks smart in the early morning sun. Introduced as one of seven Bristol VRs for use in the Plymouth Joint Services network, it was the last VR to operate in the Plymouth and South-East Cornwall area. In the late 1980s, it was converted for use on the Torpoint Ferry, with the rear engine panelling cut away to improve clearance.

Under the watchful eye of Smeaton's Tower, *Henry Winstanley* heads towards the seafront. Quite the matching pair in their striking red and white stripes.

Leyland Titan PD2 *Sir Francis Drake* in its latest crisp, cream livery 'sails' past Smeaton's Tower.

It may say Tate Gallery on the window by the half cab, but this splendid example of a London Transport bus, restored to its 1958-1960 appearance, is enjoying a day at the seaside. It is seen passing the three-tier Belvedere which is to the seaward side of Plymouth Hoe, and was built in 1891.

London Transport 1963 AEC Routemaster, 449 CLT, takes its passengers on a bit of seafront sightseeing with the walls of Plymouth Citadel to the left and Mount Batten across the waters of The Sound.

The conductor waits to see if there are any more passengers to join London Transport 1951 Leyland 7RT, LYF 104, before embarking on a trip around The Hoe.

Passing the former Grand Hotel, Bournemouth Corporation 1960 Leyland Titan PD3 heads along Elliot Street as it approaches The Hoe. One of 30 built as part of Bournemouth Corporation's trolley bus replacement, it was an unusual design based on their trolley buses with dual staircase, front entrance and rear exit. Used for many years as a museum, it was bought for preservation in 2007 after long term storage.

Originally a London Transport bus, this 1976 Bristol LH6L, KJD 413P, was sold to Tally Ho! Kingsbridge in 1982 where it was used as a school bus. The last of many LHs used by Tally Ho! before entering preservation in 2006, it is seen here coming off Plymouth Hoe as a ship heads out across the sparkling waters of Plymouth Sound.

On a blustery afternoon, heritage 1956 Leyland Titan PD2, MCO 658, owned by Plymouth CityBus, is viewed from the steps of the Belvedere as it heads towards West Hoe and its small harbour. Note the gathering of parked scooters.

1960 Leyland Atlantean PDR1/1, TCO 537, emerges from the bustle of The Barbican. Now far more of a marina than the fishing harbour it once was, flats dominate the skyline where there were once warehouses. The Mayflower Steps, from where the Pilgrim Fathers are reputed to have left for America, is bottom right.

The Leyland Atlantean heads along Madeira Road towards The Hoe. In the background is Queen Anne's Marina, and to the left is the sweeping roof of the National Marine Aquarium. The bus was new in June 1960 to Plymouth City Transport as one of the original batch of rear-engined buses delivered to the company.

EXETER DAY AND NIGHT

Devon General 1961 'Sea Dog' *Admiral Blake*, MSJ 499, comes off Western Way, passing Paris Street as it heads for Exeter Bus and Coach Station.

1948 Leyland Titan, HFJ 144, having left the bus station, travels down Paris Street with part of the expansive Princesshay shopping precinct visible at the top.

1956 Leyland Titan PD2 in Devon General livery, LRV 992, is at the city centre crossroads where Paris Street meets Sidwell Street and High Street. Devon General first operated open top buses in 1919, then reintroduced them on tourist routes in 1955. New buses introduced in 1961 were known as 'Sea Dogs' because of the names they were given. But they were later replaced in 1977 by Bristol VRs with names of warships.

1929 Maudslay ML3B, FJ 6154, was one of the first buses purchased by Exeter Corporation to act as feeders to the tram routes. Here it is, in pristine preserved condition, meeting the general public for the first time at the West Country Historic Omnibus and Transport Trust (WHOTT) 12th Historic Vehicle Rally at West Point in 2014.

The Maudslay bus was withdrawn from regular duties in 1938. It ended up being a control point for a private air strip, remaining partly hidden in a barn, until 1966. The vehicle is in the care of WHOTT whose members have restored it sympathetically back to its original 1929 specification.

1938 Leyland Tiger TS8, EFJ 666, passes along Crediton High Street en route to the Exeter Twilight Vintage Bus Running Day.

1956 Guy Arab IV, TFJ 808, leads 1958 Leyland PD2, VFJ 995, as both City of Exeter buses head through Crediton towards their old stomping ground for the twilight event.

With the sixteenth century tower of the Church of St John the Baptist in the background, 1957 Guy Arab IV, UFJ 296, stops in the centre of the village of Broadclyst.

Southern National 1951 Bristol LL6B, LTA 958, City of Exeter 1958 Leyland PD2, VFJ 995, and Bath Services 1959 Bristol LD6G Lodekka, 969 EHW, line up at Exeter Bus and Coach Station.

A fine trio of single deckers ready to go: 1950 Daimler CVD6, JFJ 873; 1938 Leyland Tiger TS8, EFJ 666; 1950 Daimler CVD6, JFJ 875.

New in 1958, Leyland PD2, VFJ 995, waits for the lights to change at the junction with Paris Street and High Street. The rain-soaked streets give everything a magical glow.

Having just left the bus station, 1957 Guy Arab IV, UFJ 296, embarks on the five mile run out to the village of Broadclyst north-east of Exeter.

Parked outside
Exeter St David's
Station, 1959 Bristol
LD6G Lodekka, 969
EHW, awaits its next
duty. This will be a
circular service from
the Paris Street bus
station via Heavitree
and Whipton Barton.

Greens in a row at
St David's with 1957
Guy Arab IV, UFJ
296, 1938 Leyland
Tiger TS8, EFJ 666,
and Bath Services
1959 Bristol LD6G
Lodekka, 969 EHW.

Doesn't that inviting glow emanating from 1963 Leyland Titan PD2A, 86 GFJ, just make you want to step inside? There is nothing more atmospheric than the interior of a vintage bus on a wet night.

An almost timeless scene as Exeter Corporation 1938 Leyland Tiger TS8, EFJ 666, and City of Exeter 1957 Guy Arab, UFJ 296, wait outside Exeter St David's Station. On some services, letters were used to identify routes to avoid confusion with the numbered Devon General country services.

Swishing through the wet streets of Exeter, 1963 Leyland PD2A, 86 GFJ, stylishly evokes a bygone era of public transport in the city as it sets out on route 8 to Broadclyst.

Heading off on route K to the Exeter suburb of Pennsylvania, 1938 Leyland Tiger TS8, EFJ 666, reaches the top of Paris Street.

Under the bright lights of John Lewis, 1959 Bristol LD6G Lodekka, 969 EHW, heads up the High Street. After being part of the Bath Services fleet, it became a staff bus at British Aerospace Filton before being preserved.

Carmel Coaches
1950 Albion Victor, LOD 495, is a delight to look at, spotlit by the lights of Exeter Bus and Coach Station. New to Way & Son of Crediton, it was sold for preservation after 21 years of service, and now earns its keep with Carmel Coaches based at Northlew, Devon.

AROUND WINKLEIGH

Going towards Winkleigh is Exeter Corporation Transport 1956 Guy Arab IV, TFJ 808, passing Townsend Corner.

Entering the centre of Winkleigh is W. Alexander & Sons Ltd, 1953 Leyland Titan PD2/12, DWG 917. Seen below the fleet number plate is a small plate with the letters 'BN' which stood for Bannockburn depot.

1929 Burlingham bodied Leyland Lioness LTB1 charabanc, DM 6228, squeezes through the narrow streets of Winkleigh. It was one of six Lionesses with all-weather convertible bodies new to White Rose Motor Services, Rhyl, passing to Crossville Motor Services in 1930.

Owner Dan Shears negotiates the tight turns as he weaves his Guy Arab IV into the centre of Winkleigh.

With roof pulled over due to the threat of inclement weather, Leyland Lioness, DM 6228, pauses in the centre of Winkleigh. The charabanc was exported to Jersey Motor Transport and, during the German occupation, it was hidden in a bricked-up tunnel to prevent it being used by occupying forces. Returning to the mainland in 1958, it has been restored to original livery.

1958 Exeter Corporation Transport Leyland PD2, VFJ 995, waits for custom in Winkleigh Square.

Thatch and cob walls give an atmospheric sense of rural Devon as the 1956 Guy Arab IV leaves the village.

Leyland PD2, KGK 529, was in the London Transport fleet from 1949 until 1964. It was then used for driver training until 1970 when it entered preservation. Here it journeys along the A3124 with Winkleigh's Second World War aerodrome legacy evident with the wartime control tower in the background.

A dash of blue with W. Alexander & Sons Ltd's 1953 Leyland Titan PD2/12.

The yellow of 1959 Leyland PD3, YLJ 147, catches the low autumn sun on one of the last trips of the day.

Some evocative North Devon holiday destinations on the blinds of 1950 Western National Bristol K6B, KUO 972.

Lovingly restored at the West of England Transport Collection is this splendid 1927 Austin 20, U0 2331, which was originally used by the Sidmouth coach company, Dagworthy.

An abundance of sunshine yellow greets the observer with this re-homed fleet of Bournemouth Corporation Transport buses. Nearest is 1960 Leyland PD3/1, 8154 EL, in the close company of single deck Leyland Royal Tiger, NLJ 272, and 1964 Leyland Atlantean PDR1, AEL 170B.

It's a case of seeing double doubles at Winkleigh. A pair of Devon Generals, 1965 AEC Regent V, CTT 513C, and 1957 AEC Regent V, VDV 817, are keeping company with a pair of Plymouth City Transport buses, ADR 813, new to the fleet in 1938 but receiving its present L53R Leyland body in 1953, and 1946 Leyland PD1, CJY 299.

This Leyland Tiger TS7, JA 7591, heading along mid-Devon roads, was built in 1937 and entered service with Stockport Corporation. It was later passed to the Welfare Department and carried a cream and green livery. It was restored to its original colours.

The Leyland Tiger cuts a dash sprinting along the open road of the B3217. This was one of several vehicles used in the filming of the 1999 movie 'Angela's Ashes' with Robert Carlyle and Emily Watson. Filmed in Ireland, it was give false Irish registration plates and livery. It was painted with Great Southern Railway ensignia which can be seen in this image.

1938 Leyland Tiger TS8, EFJ 666, passes over the level crossing at Eggesford Station. The station was opened by the North Devon Railway in 1854 and in steam days would have once seen sections of the Atlantic Coast Express and Devon Belle passing through.

Having met the Exeter to Barnstaple train, the Southern National 1951 Bristol LL6B, LTA 958, which has a 37-seat Duple coach body, heads for home.

Looking resplendent in Bournemouth Corporation Transport yellow, 1949 Leyland Tiger PS2/3, JLJ 403, with its Burlingham full fronted coachwork, leaves Eggesford.

On its service from Eggesford to Winkleigh, 1938 Leyland Tiger TS8 passes the turning to Wembworthy at Speakes Cross.

Southern National 1951 Bristol LL6B heads towards Winkleigh on one of the timed coach connections with Eggesford Station.

EXETER TO PLYMOUTH CAVALCADE

Cutting a dash as it enters Chudleigh is Bristol LS6G (OTT 98). It is taking part in the Exeter to Plymouth bus and coach stations farewell cavalcade on Saturday, 16 July 2016. The coach entered service in 1953 with Southern National Omnibus Company Ltd in Royal Blue livery for express services. Following on behind is 1954 Bristol LS6G, OTT 85, a Southern National touring coach used as a Royal Blue 'Relief' on summer weekends.

Passing under the bunting at Chudleigh is 49-seat Bedford Plaxton Panorama coach, CCG 704C, built in 1965 for King Alfred Motor Services, with a Bristol Greyhound in hot pursuit.

In original cream and red livery, 1965 Bristol MW6G/ECW, BHU 92C, Bristol Greyhound, adopts a slower pace in Ashburton as it negotiates what was once, before dual carriageways and bypasses, the main road to the west. The town mayor is in his regalia for local festivities and not to greet the unexpected spectacle of vintage buses!

Heading through Ashburton, 1950 Bristol L6B, NAE 3, negotiates a bustling East Street. It was one of three luxury coaches delivered to Bristol Tramways for tours and excursions, as well as express coach services between Bristol and London, and across the Associated Motorways network.

It's just like the old days of coach travel as the once familiar livery of Grey Cars graces Plymouth's Bretonside Bus Station. This 1963 AEC Reliance was originally used as a directors' special coach and also to take the Torquay United Football Club team to away games until 1969.

A fine line-up for the last hurrah at Bretonside Bus Station before it is annihilated under a modern complex of cinema and restaurants. Devon General Sea Dog Admiral Blake, MSJ 499, is with fellow Devon General 1956 AEC Regent Mark V, ROD 765, 1960 Leyland Atlantean Henry Winstanley, STK 131T, and Bournemouth Corporation 1960 Leyland Titan PD3, 8159 EL. To the left of Charles Cross Church is the tilted architecture of Drake Circus Shopping Mall.

Royal Blues on parade as an LS6G Bristol, built in 1953, and a 1966 Bristol MW6G make their regal presence known at Plymouth Bus Station.

Plymouth City Transport 1948 Crossley DD42-5, DJY 965, poses with Leyland Atlantean PDR1/1, TCO 537. New in June 1960 to Plymouth City Transport, the Atlantean was one of the original batch of rear-engined buses delivered to the company. Marking time on this final event is the clock on top of the Royal Bank of Scotland Group.

A seemingly thriving Plymouth Bretonside Bus Station with a cross-generation range of buses.

A glorious overview as Grey Cars AEC Reliance, 1 RDV, pulls up in front of a grand display of public transport.

Embarking on a jolly around the city is Yelloway AEC Reliance 760, WDK 562T.

1980 Leyland Leopard, FDV 803V, in Royal Blue/National livery comes up from Bretonside Bus Station and negotiates the St Andrew's Roundabout with the imposing Royal Bank of Scotland behind.

An impressive line-up of Royal Blues marks the last day of Exeter Bus and Coach Station's coach facilities.

Having the poignant honour of being the last coach to depart from Exeter Bus and Coach Station is Colin Billington's 1951 Royal Blue Bristol LL6B, LTA 729.

MIKE'S BUS

It's a long way from the old Theatre Royal, Plymouth, but this 1946 Plymouth City Transport PD1, CJY 299, looks quite at home on Dartmoor with the peak of Hare Tor rising 1,742ft above sea level in the distance. Owner Michael Bozanitz is driving it from its winter residence at Winkleigh to its summer home near Plymouth.

The PD1 began its life in 1946 when Plymouth City Transport ordered 15 PD1 buses. Withdrawn from service in 1960, it was rescued by Colin Shears in 1969 and brought to Winkleigh, having the distinction of being the first Plymouth City Transport vehicle to be preserved. CJY 299 was purchased by Michael Bozanitz in 2014 and a full restoration was carried out. It is seen here, taking a well-earned breather outside the Bedford Hotel, Tavistock, before heading on to Plymouth.

TAVISTOCK TO PRINCETOWN

1947 Bristol L6B Wilts & Dorset Motor Services, EMW 284, which was withdrawn in 1962, is seen having just crossed the River Plym en route for Yelverton followed by Western National 1962 Bristol SUL4A, 275 KTA. Both are seen at Cadover Bridge, a popular Dartmoor beauty spot, particularly in less inclement weather.

Re-enacting a Tavistock 'Day out in 1968', rebodied Bristol LL Southern National, JUO 983, passes along the dip at Merrivale on the Tavistock to Princetown run. To the right is the Dartmoor Inn and, above, the spoil tip from the former Merrivale granite quarry which closed in 1997.

Accessing the scenic delights of Dartmoor demands some stiff climbs, as rebodied Bristol LL is experiencing as it slogs up the B3357 from Merrivale on service 113. Staple Tor dominates the horizon.

It's the wild open moors and tors as Bristol LS6G, OTT 85, heads towards Princetown from Yelverton. Regular visitors to Tavistock, these vehicles were the mainstay of Western and Southern National's tours throughout the 1950s and were also used to duplicate Royal Blue services on summer weekends. The trackbed of the former railway line from Yelverton to Princetown can be seen on the right.

No time to sample a pint of real ale at the Dartmoor Inn, Merrivale, as rebodied Bristol LL6B Southern National, JUO 983, heads past towards Tavistock. On the skyline is the FM and television transmitter at North Hessary Tor which has a 643ft high mast.

Princetown is the highest village within the Dartmoor National Park, and one of the highest in the United Kingdom at around 1,430ft above sea level. Taking a well-earned rest, having completed the demanding service 113 from Tavistock, is Western National Bristol LWL5G, LTA 772, seen here parked near the Jubilee Memorial.

On approaching Tavistock, Bristol FLF6G, 468 FTT, passes the statue of Tavistock's most famous son, Sir Francis Drake. When new, the bus operated from Camborne depot, but was transferred to South Devon in 1972, working mainly from Plymouth and Totnes depots. It was sold for preservation in 1981.

Carmel Coaches' Albion, LOD 495, arrives at Lamerton with a trip from Tavistock bus station.

ROYAL BLUES ON TOUR

A trio of Royal Blues in Tavistock with 1951 Bristol LL6B half-cab, LTA 729, heading past the Bedford Hotel, followed by 1961 Bristol MW6G, 56 GUO. Meanwhile, Bristol LS6G, OTT 98, built in 1953, parks up for a short break.

With Tavistock Town Hall behind, Midland Red BMMO C5 coach, 780 GHA, built in 1959, passes through Bedford Square on a quiet Sunday morning.

Turning a few heads as it passes through Bedford Square is Bristol MW6G, EDV 505D. Built in 1966, it was in service with Western National and based at Plymouth, and given Royal Blue fleet names in between 1970-71.

You would not go thirsty in Okehampton when this picture was taken, as Bristol LL6B, LTA 729, and 1980 Leyland Leopard, FDV 803V, in Royal Blue National livery, pass between the White Hart Hotel and the London Inn.

Midland Red BMMO C5, 780 GHA, passes through the village of Tedburn St Mary en route to Exeter.

After a light shower of rain, 1951 Bristol LL6B half-cab, LTA 729, on a Royal Blue run to Cornwall, heads towards the centre of Crediton with the grounds of the Church of the Holy Cross behind.

Travelling along Tavistock's Plymouth Road, 1962 Bristol SUL4A, 275 KTA, slows for the pedestrian crossing. With a little imagination you could almost picture that iconic Beatles' Abbey Road album cover with John, Paul, George and Ringo striding across the zebra lines.

Royal Blue Bristol RELH6G, OTA 632G, sweeps down Kinterbury Street from St Andrew's Cross roundabout and into Plymouth's Bretonside.

It's high tide on the wide waters of the River Taw at Barnstaple as Royal Blue, 1960 Bristol MW6G, 625 DDV, passed the Imperial Hotel heading towards The Square.

The Barnstaple town clock says 10.25 and the convoy of Royal Blues are on schedule. Here they will make a brief stop before continuing to Ilfracombe and on to Minehead. Driving over Long Bridge spanning the Taw is 1953 Bristol LS6G, OTT 98.

The 'Blues' have reached Ilfracombe with 1952 Royal Blue Bristol LS6G, MOD 973, heading along The Promenade towards the harbour area. Behind is the conical shape of the Landmark Theatre, and the imposing building on the hill which was once a Victorian hotel.

The sea in the Bristol Channel is less than blue as 1964 Crossville Motor Services Bristol ECW, AFM 105B, heads along The Promenade and past the seaward rock face of Capstone Hill.

1969 Bristol RELH6G, OTA 632G, leaves Ilfracombe for Minehead, the next leg of the 2018 annual south-west tour, and draws some admiring glances along the way.

DESTINATION DARTMOUTH

After the Kingsbridge Vintage Bus Running Day, some vehicles would embark on an organised outing the day after. On this occasion, they have lined up at Slapton Sands prior to heading on to Dartmouth.

Heading the 'convoy' up along the coast road from Slapton Sands towards Stoke Fleming is 1939 Bristol L5G, DOD 518. This bus continued in service until 1961 and was based at Kingsbridge depot from May to October 1959.

The splendid multi-coloured range of liveries make up this line-up at Dartmouth, headed by Wilts & Dorset Bristol L6B, EMW 284. The chassis was new in 1947 and the body was rebuilt to the present style in 1957, with the vehicle withdrawn in 1962.

R.I.H LONGMAN
MANAGING   DIRECTOR
8 ENDLESS ST SALISBURY

The picturesque properties of Dartmouth are viewed from beneath the canopy of the Bristol L6B. One of the town's earliest buildings, the seventeenth century traditional English coaching inn, the Royal Castle Hotel, is seen across the harbour.

TOTNES

Making an early morning dash out of Totnes on a feeder service to the Kingsbridge Vintage Bus Running Day is 1947 Scarlet Pimpernel Motors of Minehead, Leyland Tiger PS1, JYC 855. The Harrington tail fin is certainly an eye-catching embellishment.

Under the watchful eye of St Mary's Church at the top of Fore Street, 1953 Leyland Tiger PS2, EHL 336, swings left towards Totnes Bridge.

Used at the Western National Totnes depot for most of its life, it is appropriate that 1945 Bristol K6A, FTT 704, is rostered on this particular Kingsbridge service. The bus is seen departing from The Plains, after which it will cross the River Dart on Totnes Bridge.

The Maltsters Arms, Harbertonford, looks an inviting hostelry as the Scarlet Pimpernel, JYC 855, heads towards Totnes along the A381. This superbly restored coach entered a life of preservation in 1992.

Rolling into Totnes is 1950 Leyland PS1/1, LFM 302, originally used on the Coastal Express from Liverpool around the North Wales coast and sold into preservation in 1970. Following behind is the Scarlet Pimpernel.

It's a stiff climb out of Totnes on the A381 but Totnes depot stalwart Western National 1945 Bristol K6A, FTT 704, takes the climb steadily in its stride.

MODBURY, BIGBURY-ON-SEA AND SALCOMBE

Pulling up for a short stop in Church Street, Modbury, is Western National 1951 Bristol LWL5G, LTA 772. In the background is the Exeter Inn, dating from the fourteenth century, the oldest surviving inn in the town, and a one-time popular meeting place of the Royalists.

A **perfect** pastoral scene as 1950 Bristol KS5G, LTA 813, takes the road to Bigbury-on-Sea. The fields have been harvested and the distinctive spire of St Lawrence Church, Bigbury, can be seen protruding above the tree line.

1978 Bristol VRT, VDV 121S, which was withdrawn in 2003, climbs the steep Folly Hill away from Bigbury-on-Sea, and the island of Burgh Island with its Art Deco hotel. When the tide is in, visitors are transported to the island by means of a sea tractor.

1949 Tilling-Stevens, GOU 732, seen with the Burgh Island Hotel behind. In the 1930s, this location was a bolt hole for some of London's rich and famous, including Noel Coward. The island served as the inspirational setting for Devon author Agatha Christie's novel *And Then There Were None*, and for the Hercule Poirot mystery, *Evil Under the Sun*. The coach was run by Altonian for 28 years. It is seen in a fictitious livery based on that of Wolverhampton Corporation.

Passing Holy Trinity Church, Salcombe, is 1946 AEC Regal, HTT 487. The bus ended up derelict in a field before being rescued for preservation.

Grey Cars 1963 AEC Reliance, 1 RDV, crosses the River Avon at Aveton Gifford with a return trip from Bigbury-on-Sea.

AROUND KINGSBRIDGE

Winding through the back streets of Kingsbridge is 1948 Bristol L6B, KHY 383, which was new to Bristol Omnibus Co. After withdrawal, it went to a contractor in Bath before being preserved.

Swinging into Kingsbridge bus station is 1962 Bristol SUL4A, 286 KTA, which was originally a Southern National coach based at Bideford, North Devon. In 1979, it was sold on and subsequently worked on Guernsey. It returned to the mainland in 1979 and was restored in Guernsey Motor Co's Deltatours livery.

Originally in service with Western National, 1951 Bristol LWL5G, LTA 772, transferred to Southern National in 1959 and was based at Weymouth. Sold into preservation in 1968, it was, in 2013, repainted back into its original guise. Seen here returning to town on the Loddiswell service.

1927 Guy FBB, YF 714, bus was built for the Great Western Railway and entered service at the GWR Penzance Depot on transport duties linked to the rail terminus. Several years later, it came under the operation of Western National and was painted in the company's livery of green with a cream waist band. It is believed that the bus was withdrawn and sold in 1931.

The bus was converted to a caravan and moved to Perranporth and used as holiday accommodation. In 1972, two enthusiasts purchased the bus. Miraculously the major mechanical components remained with the vehicle. Restoration began in 2000 and was completed in 2011 and it is seen here at Kingsbridge in all its restored GWR glory in 2013.

This delightful Southern National 1934 Dennis Mace, BTA 59, was based in North Devon, principally Ilfracombe. In 1952 it was sold to the coxswain of the Appledore lifeboat. It was converted to a mobile caravan, and later sold to a family in the Midlands who used it for holidays until 1985. The vehicle passed through six preservation owners before being fully restored.

1934 Bristol J, AHU 803, heads along the A379 towards West Charleton with a full load of passengers eager for their first glimpse of the coast.

1951 Leyland Titan PD2, MTT 640, heads towards Kingsbridge along Embankment Road. The Devon General bus ended up being sold to a building contractor in Durham for staff transport. It was acquired for preservation in 1975.

The tide is coming in at Bowcombe Creek as a single decker crosses New Bridge.

1950 Bristol K6B, KUO 972, heads over Bowcombe Creek. This bus was a low bridge type and worked in Cornwall from the Newquay depot. Sold in 1970, it went to a farmer in Kent for transporting fruit pickers. It became part of the West of England Transport Collection at Winkleigh where it was restored.

Crossing Bowcombe Creek. This 1934 Bristol J was built by Bristol Tramways and Carriage Company as a private hire coach, and was originally a petrol-engined vehicle, being converted to diesel in 1947.

Reflections as 1951 Leyland Titan PD2, MTT 640, Devon General crosses Bowcombe Bridge. The bus spent much of its time in the Tiverton/Exeter area.

1940 Bristol L5G, DOD 518, entered service in Plymouth. It later transferred to Kingsbridge until 1959 when it was withdrawn and became a crew room at Launceston. Here it is in splendid preserved fettle heading towards Kingsbridge with Bowcombe Creek in the background.

Just fitting through the narrow lanes, verdant with summer bracken growth, is 1979 Bristol LHS6L, FDV 790V, heading for East Portlemouth.

Here it is climbing up from East Portlemouth with the estuary town of Salcombe in the distance.

1962 Bristol SUL4A, 286 KTA, in striking Deltatours livery, crosses the River Avon near Loddiswell on its way to Kingsbridge.

Easing through the narrow streets of Loddiswell, with a smart piece of thatch on the cob cottage, 1951 Leyland 7RT, LYF 104, is a long way from its London roots, and routes! This London Transport vehicle was a tram replacement originally based at Wandsworth garage. It was withdrawn and sold in 1963.

HOPE COVE, MALBOROUGH AND THURLESTONE

It is an idyllic summer's day as Daimler CVD6, JFJ 873, delivered to Exeter Corporation in 1950, departs from Inner Hope for Kingsbridge. It was withdrawn in 1966 and entered preservation three years later.

Western National 'twins', their registrations separated by just two numbers, wait to depart from this attractive location at Inner Hope. 1960 Bristol SUS4A, 672 COD, a type designed for narrow and lightly laden routes, was based at Totnes before being transferred to Penzance. Also, 1960 Bristol SUS4A, 675 COD, entered service at Totnes but spent much of its career working out of Penzance and Helston. After withdrawal, the bus spent 27 years with a church in London, entering preservation in 2000.

1951 Bedford SBG, PPH 698, passes Saint Clements Church, Hope Cove, with the headland of Bolt Tail across the bay in the background. Its present owner had the bus converted back to petrol in 1999 after running with a diesel engine for 30 years.

Taking the road to Inner Hope, with the spread of spacious coastal properties leading down to Outer Hope below, is 1962 Bristol SUL4A, 811 BWR. New to West Yorkshire Road Car Co, it was sold to a school in 1972, then to BP Chemicals at Saltend Refinery, Hull, for internal works transport. It passed into preservation in 1983.

Outer Hope with the sea mist rolling in as 1950 Daimler CVD6, JFJ 873, City of Exeter half-cab prepares to leave Hope Cove. The Hope and Anchor stands invitingly behind, with the Cottage Hotel above and Mouthwell Sands just beyond the houses.

It might say Mystery Tour on the front of 1954 Bristol LS6G, OTT 85, as it heads through the village of Malborough, but the window sticker on the Southern National gives the game away – this coach is off to Hope Cove. Mainly based at Weymouth it was used on weekday tours and as a Royal Blue 'Relief' coach at weekends.

1950 Daimler CVD6 City of Exeter passes the Grade I listed Church of All Saints at Malborough. The building, with its magnificent spire, is the highest point of the village.

Squeezing through the narrows at Malborough is 1946 AEC Regal, Devon General, which is a representative of the company's post war single deck fleet of half-cabs.

Pictured previously in Winkleigh with the hood down, here 1929 Burlingham-bodied Leyland Lioness charabanc, DM 6228, enjoys pure South Hams sunshine on a glorious September day as it climbs up through Thurlestone on the return run to Kingsbridge. The Lioness is passing a charming thatch-roofed dwelling at Rock Hill Corner and the turning for Bantham.

The clock on All Saints Church glints in the late morning sun as 1951 Bedford SBG heads through Thurlestone heading to the popular coastal golf club where it will turn around. New to Epsom Coaches for touring work, it remained there until 1956 when it became the property of Heard's Coaches, Hartland, North Devon. It was purchased from here by its present owner in 1997 and restored to original livery.

TORCROSS AND SLAPTON SANDS

1948 AEC Regal III, CFK 340, approaches Torcross, with the waters of Slapton Ley National Nature Reserve mirroring the hills in the background. The coach carries the original livery of the fleet of Burnham's of Worcester.

While dark clouds threaten rain, the AEC Regal III makes a photographic stop in the village centre of Torcross.

Could this bus be on a summer holiday from the city? London Transport 1951 Leyland 7RT, LYF 104, is driving along Slapton Sands, enjoying a sojourn by the blue sea and blue sky of Devon.

Maybe having taken the wrong turning for Weston-super-Mare would be a bonus for passengers aboard the 1934 Bristol J, Bristol Tramways and Carriage Company. This trip is a perfect way to enjoy the scenery along the A379 between the waters of Slapton Ley and the golden beach of Slapton Sands. The bus remained in service until 1958, when it was sold to the Nailsworth Boys Club prior to restoration to its 1947 condition.

Leyland Titan PD2, MCO 658, *Sir Francis Drake,* circumnavigates the waters of Slapton Ley, the largest natural freshwater lake in south-west England, on the approach to Torcross. It is seen here in its earlier Plymouth City Transport livery before being painted cream.

Climbing up from the beauty spot of Blackpool Sands is 1949 Bedford OB, MHU 49, with the alluring waters of Landcombe Cove below. This bus was Bristol Tramways' first new post-war Bedford and their first OB bus. It saw service for 18 years on Mid Wales Motorways, Newtown, before passing into preservation.

Western National 1945 Bristol K6A, FTT 704, approaches Slapton Ley, a National Nature Reserve rich in flora and fauna.

Dominating the far end of the road that divides Slapton Ley from Slapton Sands is the Slapton Monument. The memorial was presented by the United States Army to the people of the South Hams, 'who generously left their homes and their lands to provide a battle practice area for the successful assault in Normandy in June 1944…' Seen passing by is preserved Huddersfield Joint Omnibus Committee 1945 Daimler CWA6, CCX 777, which was withdrawn from service in 1967 and was purchased for preservation that year.

All is serene along this picturesque section of the A379 as 1960 Bristol FLF6G, 468 FTT, heads towards Slapton village. The *Cornish Times* was prone to add the odd yet eye-catching eccentricity to its advertising, hence the line that the newsprint 'Also wraps whelks'.

There is hardly a ripple on the blue waters of Start Bay as Western National 1945 Bristol K6A, FTT 704, heads towards Torcross. On such a perfect autumnal day it is hard to imagine the damage storms can do to this fragile shingle bar that separates the freshwater lake of Slapton Ley from the sea.

LODDISWELL

1933 Bristol H, FJ 8967, Western National, passes under the bridge of the former Kingsbridge branch line at Loddiswell. This vehicle was always a South Devon vehicle, spending its operational life working from Dartmouth, Kingsbridge and Plymouth depots until withdrawal in 1957.

The California Country Inn at California Cross looks very tempting but it is not yet opening time as the Western National passes on the B3196.